Behind the Scenes

A Different Kind of Christmas Tale

Amarilys Gacio Rassler

Illustrated by Deborah Smith

Name: Rassler , Amarilys Gacio
Title: *Behind the Scenes, A Different Kind of Christmas Tale* , Amarilys Gacio Rassler
Illustrations: Deborah Smith
Interior and cover layouts: Robert Ousnamer

ISBN: 978-1-955309-82-0

Subjects: Books › Children's Books › Holidays & Celebrations › Christmas
2. Books › Children's Books › Religions › Christianity › General
3. Books › Religions › Christianity › Inspirational

Published byEABooks Publishing
a division of Living Parables of Central Florida, Inc.
eabookspublishing.com

To the One who loves me most,
Happy birthday, Jesus!

And to my Esposo, family, and Bistro Group,
I love you.

Thanks, and recognition go to Word Weavers,
Tampa Writers Alliance, Florida Writers Association,
and to EABooks Publishing

Thank you, Cheri, Lisa, Jeanette, Rebecca, Debbie, Bob and Monica
You made this dream possible.

Mil gracias go to
Ana Rettig, my prayer partner for forty years,
te quiero.

****

To

_____

From

_____

Message

_____

_____

_____

_____

****

Elizabeth shivered as she pulled back a strand of gray hair. With shaky fingers she tucked it under her raggedy shawl while her heart sank fast into a hollow hole. She traipsed over twigs and roots that pressed against her thin-soled sandals. Her arms ached from pushing away branch after branch that impeded her getting somewhere. But where? It seemed like hours of walking through a dark, lonely forest. With every step the wind blew harder. It appeared to feed on her movements like an angry ogre determined to blow her away.

Suddenly, a force lifted her high off the ground and twirled her in multiple circles. Elizabeth clutched her scarf. Her vision clouded. She shut her eyes and gasped. She rubbed her chest, soothing a pressure. Was this her time to die?

Her feet descended on something soft like lambs' sheared wool. Thick fog surrounded her. She strained to see, to make out shapes at her sides. The vapor-like substance around her lifted as if peeled away by a gentle hand.

People stood in line close by. Quietly. In line for what? Was this a dream? Where was she? She was too old for this. Her heart had been giving her troubles, and recently her knees throbbed after kneeling to pray. "Jehovah-Jireh, my provider, Most Holy One, please wake me up."

An old man with a peppered beard pulled on a little boy's tunic. "Speak up and see what you get. Hurry up. There're many behind you!"

The child observed the harsh countenance marked with narrow tracks on leather-like skin. He wiped wet crystals out of his huge brown eyes and nodded. Elizabeth huffed. Her hands balled.

A long window opened in front of the boy. "Your name, please." A glowing face leaned forward grinning. The figure's smile shimmered as if shooting rainbows.

"Joshua. But Mother calls me Josh."

"I see. Where do you live?" The glowing figure raised a glimmering hand and a book appeared upon it. He flipped pages.

Joshua's brows knitted together. "Bethlehem, sir."

Elizabeth exhaled. Her body loosened. What a nice little fellow.

The glowing one winked. "Affirmative. It's all here. And let's see … what is it that you want?"

Elizabeth listened while studying her surroundings. People in long garments stood before her and behind her. She recognized no one.

She focused on the boy. For sure he must be scared without his mother there. She tried to move closer to him, but her feet were rooted. Her heart shrank, like an old, withered fig. And yet, he stood firm. He was brave. Oh, how she loved to see that young one's courage. A little boy. If only she'd had a boy of her own. Just one little boy. Elizabeth stared at the child. She wiped away an errant tear.

The boy scratched at the band around his matted hair. "Sir, I want to make music for a king. But I have no instrument."

The figure behind the window put his book down. "I see. Does it matter the instrument?" Joshua shook his head.

Loud drums thrummed around them. Above them lights flashed. In an instant straps appeared around Joshua's neck attached to a small drum. Two wooden sticks in his hands."

Joshua laughed. His eyes lit like lanterns.

"Go, play, Joshua. The King is coming." The figure behind the window extended his glowing hand and ruffled the child's hair.

Joshua tapped the drum with a stick. "How? What?"

"Practice, Josh. Like this, parum pum, pum, pum."

Joshua nodded and smiled.

Elizabeth held her breath as another tear escaped. Lights flashed again. She blinked. And in an instant the little boy was gone. Elizabeth swallowed hard. A familiar emptiness echoed through her.

"Move out of the way, Melchee. You're stepping on my bunion."

Elizabeth held back a giggle. To her right three elderly gentlemen of different shapes, wearing expensive robes and silken turbans, pushed toward the glass window.

The window opened with a cymbal-like chime. The familiar glowing face lifted a corner of his mouth. "Gentlemen, you will have no power of petition here if you argue."

The men stared at each other. One said, "Begging your pardon, Gaspar. Didn't mean to step on you." The tall, lanky, cinnamon-skinned gentleman with a full moustache bowed and then straightened. "Please, let us remain within character for this mission. This is serious. I haven't been Melchee since childhood. Melchior is my name."

"Melchior it is." Gaspar, short and rounded, bowed low and popped an almond into his mouth. "Let's finish the business at hand."

The figure at the window cleared his throat. "Melchior and Gaspar." The glowing face leaned toward the unnamed man who watched with arms crossed. "And you, sir, what is your name?"

"Balthasar." The handsome man with dark twinkling eyes, muscular build, and long gray beard, took a bow. "At your service."

"Wonderful! That is what we like to hear." The glowing figure behind the window tapped his gleaming lips with his finger. "And your place of habitation?"

Gaspar popped another almond into his mouth. "India."

Melchior stepped closer to the glass. "Persia."

Balthasar straightened his back. "Arabia. But you must know this?"

The figure behind the window winked at Balthasar and flipped through his book again. "I see it. It is all here. And you are looking for the King?"

The King? Elizabeth watched the three men as they affirmed with their chins. The eating one, still munching on almonds, seemed to glance over her way. The group so fancy, royal-like. She tucked her hair under her shawl again and pressed her palm down on her long rough garment, wishing to smooth any creases. Could they see her? She glimpsed at the people around her in queue and questioned their reality. They were so quiet. And at times as if undulating. A mirage? Elizabeth shuddered. If this was a dream, it was one she would never forget. She darted to attention at the voices up ahead.

"Well, gentlemen, your petitions have been approved. You shall see the King. However, there is a matter of the gifts you are to bring."

Melchior adjusted his tipping turban and stroked an ear decorated with a sparkling diamond. "What is the problem? Balthasar is bringing a large quantity of gold. Gold of the highest quality, fit for the most wonderful king. The heavens have spoken. The stars indicated that this is no common birth, no ordinary happening."

Gaspar tucked an almond into a small red velvet bag strapped to his waist as his rounded belly bounced with a jolly chuckle. "Because I am very partial to scents and perfumes. I shall bring the best frankincense of my beloved India. Its aroma shall fill the most exquisite rooms of his royal highness. The king will have a most pure and majestic scent fit for a deity. We await with longing to visit him at his palace."

"Those gifts are on the agenda. However, myrrh has been added to the list. If you would accept the assignment to bring these three gifts…."

Balthasar jolted into a pillar-like stance. His face transformed into a stone-sculptured frown. "Myrrh? Impossible. That is of great offense. It is embalming oil for the dead. We must not bring this to a child." He stared at the figure behind the window and shook his head.

"I am afraid it is beyond your understandings now. And it is not time yet for the explanation to be given. We will retain the assignment for someone else."

Two voices thundered. "No!" Gaspar and Melchior stood close to the glass. "For Heaven's sake no." They both glared at Balthasar. "For sure you shall go with us. Why should we question what is required of us?"

Gaspar and Melchior drew close to Balthasar, his face hidden with his hands. "This is unthinkable. May there be no prophecy intended." He wiped his eyes. "You're right. I shall do as is asked."

Melchior returned to the window. "How shall we find him?"

"You shall follow a star."

"Fire, flames, for guidance, they appear to be more appropriate, don't you think?"

Gaspar opened his velvet pouch, brought out more nuts and ate them. "Yes, fire. We have read the Hebrew Torah. Fire worked for Moses … and more than once. A star? What kind of symbol is that? It won't make a very good story. Who's going to remember a star?" Gaspar chuckled in between bites.

The lights flashed on and off. Harp music played loud and hard.

Elizabeth looked up and the three men scanned the area above them.

Balthasar turned in circles. "What's happening?" Strings continued to play in a discordant way.

The glowing face behind the window dimmed. "We, workers here, have different titles: hosts, chariots, sons of God, angels, watchers, messengers, and stars. You insulted the angel, the star, who will show you the way."

Melchior shoved an elbow into Gaspar. "Keep eating those nuts. It'll stop your mammoth foot from filling your mouth."
Balthasar rushed to the figure in the window. "We shall gladly seek the star."

The harps ceased playing and, in an instant, the three gentlemen disappeared. The glass window closed.

Suddenly, a beggar-like man in front of Elizabeth mumbled. "Speak up and see what you get, speak up and see what you get, speak up and see what you get." He groaned. "About time I got something." He plunked down by her feet and scratched his hairy arms sticking out from his burlap garment. His fingernails, caked with dirt, reached for his dark, sun-burned face and oily hair. A stench of stable animals and human sweat wafted toward Elizabeth. She buried her nose into the corner of her shawl.

The glass window opened. "Next, please."

The beggar raced to the glass. "Me."

"State your name and place of habitation, please."

"Zebulon son of Juda." The short, cork-shaped man kept rubbing his arms with his knuckles. "Where I live? I am a shepherd outside of Bethlehem. It's a hard life. Ticks, fleas, flies, maggots, you name it. And sheep are dumb, man."

The glowing figure opened his book once more. "Yes, I see here you wish to be recognized, to be affirmed and somehow remembered."

The man stopped his scratching. His blotchy arms went limp. "Is it so wrong to do something for the little people? We feed the big wheels: rabbis, priests, Pharisees, and Sadducees. Those fat cats eat our lambs with their mint jelly while leaning on their fancy cushions. They vomit out their loud burps of approval and then, those baboons act like we stink."

Elizabeth uncovered her nose fast.

"Without us, no sheep, no lambs, not one little baa sound. Look at this." Zebulon pulled back cloth and pointed to a snake-like scar on his arm. "A wild dog bite. Me? I protect my sheep."

"I hear you. Go on, I'm listening."

"The boys and me, we want to be part of something big. Just once. You got it?"

"Something bigger than yourself. Something really big."

Zebulon began scratching himself again. "Fleas, fleas, fleas."

The figure behind the window flipped through pages of his book. "Ah, here it is. You are of strong constitution, could you stand for a huge surprise? You appear not to fear?"

Zebulon stepped closer to the glass laughing. "Me, fear? I fear nothing! Bring it on. They don't call me Bulging-Chest Zeb for nothing." Zebulon pushed out his chest and patted it.

"Fine, fine." The glowing figure closed the book. "Done. We will send instructions."

"Really? That's it. You better not send scrolls … I can't read, you see."

"Do you like singing? Music?"

"Music? Sure. I don't get to hear much of it. No King Davids playing harp out there for us and the fold. You catch my drift? Are your people any good?"

"We're sending the best. Maybe I'll join them."

Elizabeth watched as Zebulon cackled, did some jumps, sprung off the ground and vanished.

The window remained opened. The glowing figure waved. "Step up, Elizabeth. You have been very patient."

Elizabeth drew near trembling. She fidgeted with strings at the end of her scarf. "Sir, is this a dream?"

"No, Elizabeth, not really. And what are dreams but bridges into another world. Step back and look up."

Elizabeth did as she was told. A huge sign she had not noticed hung over clouds with the message, Prayer Central.

"This is Heaven. You're at the Department of Received and Answered Prayers."

Elizabeth gulped down a swallow. "My prayers, sir…."

The glowing figure appeared to brighten even more. "Yes, affirmative. Elizabeth, you will conceive and have a boy."

Elizabeth buried her face in her hands and wept. "Praise … be to … to my God."

She sobbed and sobbed then lifted her eyes. "Zech, my spouse. Should I tell him?"

"No. Let us handle that. You know Zechariah. He has some rough edges."

Elizabeth affirmed with a weak smile. "You'll send him a message."

"We're sending Big G. He'll know how to handle him. He's an expert with rough edges."

"Big G?"

"Gabriel, one of our best."

"And my boy? What will he be like?"

The glowing figure puckered his lips. "Like his father, I am afraid. Even rougher. But, his personality will work for his assignment. You must call him, John. Get him to like honey. Buy him some camel pelts. Don't stop him from eating bugs." The glowing figure drummed his long golden fingers over his book. "Anything else?"

Elizabeth lingered. "Yes, do I have to go back through that forest? It was daunting and I am so old. I almost fell twice."

The glowing figure shook his head and grinned. "No. Sorry. That was the Opposition. They tried to keep you away from answered prayer. But you held on as a fine prayer warrior. Your mission is finished. There will be another way home. Shalom, Elizabeth. You are blessed."

Elizabeth bowed. "Thank you, thank you. Shalom."

She moved slowly turned away and then glanced back. A young girl stood at the glass window. A tingle ran through Elizabeth. She wanted to run to her.

"Your name, please."

"Mary. Mary of Nazareth."

Pages flipped. "And your petition?"

"Nothing, sir. I came to surrender."

"Surrender?"

"Yes, sir, please. I want to give myself to God. I want to do anything, anything He wants me to do."

"Anything?"

The End?

About The Author

Amarilys Gacio Rassler is a six time Royal Palm Literary award-winning author and speaker who writes and speaks about faith-based topics, spiritual warfare themes, and cultural Cuban subjects. She is the author of *Cuban-American, Dancing On The Hyphen*, used by Oregon State University for cultural studies and the book, *The Chairs*, a Christmas book about angels coming to a town to help a family because of an elderly couple's prayers. Amarilys writes prose and poetry, fiction, and nonfiction. Her stories and poems have been published in diverse anthologies and received awards. One of her award-winning stories, *The Rafters*, was read and acted out by actors at an improvisation theater. Words from her book, *Cuban-American, Dancing On The Hyphen*, were used in the trailer of an immigration documentary, American Dreams. Amarilys loves Christmas and enjoys writing tales about it in gratitude to the Lord for His love and mercy. She lives in Florida with her husband of fifty-three years and their much loved Jack Russell terrier, Chipper. Amarilys loves to cook Cuban food. It is her great joy to see her children, grandchildren, and friends enjoying what she makes.

www.amarilysgaciorassler.net, Facebook, Twitter, Instagram

Amarilys Rassler
Author

Deborah Smith
Illustrator

About The Illustrator

Deborah Smith's love for art was nurtured at a young age, and has developed into an award-winning, internationally sold artist. She has taken her love for Christ and her passion for art and incorporated them into her life's work as an illustrator, painter, sculptor, and art instructor.

Prior to her current vocation in book illustrating, she had a distinguished and prestigious career as a Walt Disney World Artist, Designer and Art Director. She has received many accolades and awards for her art and continues to exhibit her work throughout the Central Florida area. Deborah resides in Orlando, Florida with her husband.

"It truly is a blessing to pursue and share my passion for art. I will never tire of the joy and fulfillment it brings."

www.deborahsmithfineart.com   www.3-deborah-smith.pixels.com

www.ingramcontent.com/pod-product-compliance
Lightning Source LLC
Chambersburg PA
CBHW041127120626
46547CB00019B/2886